"Be one with your empty nest."
BUDDHA

"The times they have a-changed."
BOB DYLAN

"They'll be back, baby."
ARNOLD SCHWARZENEGGER

"Go boldly where you've never gone before."
CAPTAIN JAMES T. KIRK

"It's nothing a pint of our Empty Nest Swirl won't cure."
BEN AND JERRY

"So now what's the village supposed to do?"
HILLARY CLINTON

(What these famous people might have said about Empty Nest Syndrome had anyone bothered to ask them.)

133 Ways to Avoid Going Cuckoo When the Kids Fly the Nest

A Parent's Guide for Surviving Empty Nest Syndrome

Lauren Schaffer and
Sandy Fleischl Wasserman

THREE RIVERS PRESS • NEW YORK

Published by Three Rivers Press, New York, New York. Member of the Crown Publishing Group.

Random House, Inc. New York, Toronto, London, Sydney, Auckland
www.randomhouse.com

THREE RIVERS PRESS is a registered trademark and the Three Rivers Press colophon is a trademark of Random House, Inc.

Printed in the United States of America

Design by Lauren Dong

Illustrations by Janet Pedersen

Library of Congress Cataloging-in-Publication Data
Schaffer, Lauren.
    133 ways to avoid going cuckoo when the kids fly the nest: a parent's guide for surviving empty nest syndrome/Lauren Schaffer and Sandy Fleischl Wasserman.—1st ed.
    1. Empty nesters.   2. Empty nesters—Family relationships.
    3. Empty nesters—Psychology.   I. Title: One hundred thirty-three ways to avoid going cuckoo when the kids fly the nest.   II. Wasserman, Sandy Fleischl.   III. Title.

HQ755.83 .S33 2001
306.874—dc21

00-047964

ISBN 0-609-80700-5
10 9 8 7 6 5 4 3 2 1
First Edition

Dedicated with love to our reasons why—

Erin, Lauren, Djuna, and Jackson.

With special thanks to Elizabeth Rapoport,

our editor extraordinaire and patient mentor;

and to Steve and Tom, for picking up the slack.

CONTENTS

INTRODUCTION

A well-organized maternity ward would have handed you this book with your newborn's birth certificate. Here it is eighteen years later; it really *did* go by in the blink of an eye. The transition to empty nest status has been likened to being fired from a job you never wanted to quit; it's another kind of labor, except this time it's your heart that's having contractions. The empty nest experience can be an arduous roller-coaster ride, repeatedly hurtling you from the depths of depression to the pinnacles of unfettered joy. This trek might take three months, it might take three years; it's different for every parent. But remember, you're in this mess because of the great job you've done. Your child is ready to go out into the world and, in reality, has been gradually crawling out of the nest for years.

The committees you volunteered for, the games you attended, the fevers you treated, all make you susceptible to any of the many strains of Empty Nest Syndrome (aka ENS). And wouldn't you know it? Just when you finally need them, there are no age-old traditions to lean on, no sagacious words to pluck off the proverbial tree of wisdom. Considering child-rearing is the oldest job in the world, you'd think someone would have gotten together a self-help manual (there's one for everything else in life) to get us through this. But fear not. Although *syndrome* suggests the need for painful surgical procedures or extensive therapy, we believe you will not only survive ENS but triumphantly conquer it, with the help of our practical suggestions, ideas, and strategies.

According to our espresso-enhanced research, nothing like this book exists. We wrote it because one of us just survived Empty Nest Syndrome and the other is going to need all the help she can get to do so. We figured that at least some of the other parents of the millions of kids graduating from high school, going off to work, or joining the military could make use of the trial-by-fire experiences and solutions that have manifested themselves in our 133 essential, indispensable survival tips. This guide is organized in chapters that will help you take care of yourself when your children leave, make a fresh start, confirm that you're still a parent, prepare you for return visits, and give you hindsight for the next time around. Furthermore, our guide identifies the symptoms and suggests remediation for the eight clinical phases of ENS as defined by Schaffer and Wasserman:

1. Denial (He's still just a baby!)
2. Grief I (I'm sad, sad, sad.)
3. Acceptance (It's healthy she's leaving.)
4. Grief II (So who needs healthy?)
5. Recovery (I think I'm ready to go to a play.)

6. Grief III (Oy, I'm so sad, he was in a play.)
7. Relief (I don't have to pretend to enjoy the damned play.)
8. Glee (Hey, *I'll* be in a play!)

As you enter the realm of empty nesters, it is critical to remember that you are not engaged in an isolated, clear-cut crisis. Empty Nest Syndrome could be just one of many challenges you're facing at this time. Its impact can be exacerbated by caring for aging parents, middle-age spread, menopause, male midlife crisis, root canals, or a balloon house payment. Anthropologists tell us that traditions help us through times of change and that in many cultures, humor is used to deal with adversity. Therefore, along with our many practical and field-tested ideas, we have infused humor (sometimes irreverent) to help you keep or regain your sense of levity. It worked for us, and we hope it will help you. Enjoy and good luck!

133 Ways to Avoid Going Cuckoo When the Kids Fly the Nest

CHAPTER 1

Taking Care of Yourself *OR* From Treadmills to Tranquilizers

This is a time to control what you can, and let go of what you can't. Don't expect your kids to understand your feelings; they want *out*! You need to stay sane as they leave the nest. There's no magic fix, but the following are some don'ts and do's that have been tested in the trenches.

LAND MINES (Don'ts)

1. Don't go into your kid's room right after he leaves. This is a total setup, to be avoided no matter how you're feeling. You risk any of the following scenarios:

a. crawling into his empty bed, pulling the covers over your head, and crying for two days.

b. indulging the inadvisable urge to prematurely convert his room into an exercise room, guest room, art studio, or workshop.

c. precipitating a coronary when you see the residual mountains of trash, the piles of childhood memorabilia, cracker boxes, soda cans and molding dishes, the stacks of unreturned videos, the accumulation of unmatched shoes and mateless socks, the lost remote or cordless phone, and the complete collection of your presumed-missing CDs.

2. Don't sell the house or make a major move immediately. Your friends, neighbors, and family can be valuable support systems.

3. Don't start a diet. Need we say more?

4. Don't organize the family photo album. The pictures have been waiting in the drawer for years, possibly decades; they can wait a little longer.

5. Don't play the radio when you're feeling down—it's fraught with maudlin songs. To avoid having to pull off the road because you're sobbing hysterically, buy or rent audio books on tape. These don't have to be great literature. Get sucked into a Tony Hillerman or Agatha Christie mystery, a Tom Clancy thriller, or Tolkien's *Lord of the Rings* for a nostalgic return to the 1960s (remember Middle Earth?).

6. Don't make bedroom changes or upgrades without her involvement. If she's going to lose her room to shifting sibling logistics, or if you're planning to convert it into a sewing room, den, or bordello, be sure she takes part in the decision before she leaves. This will prevent feelings of displacement during her initial visits home.

7. Don't revisit special memory-filled places you went with your kids. During the early phases of ENS, this is emotional quicksand, unless we're talking about the orthodontist or family planning clinic.

8. Don't be a stoic. If you've eaten your weight in chocolate, you don't want to get out of bed— ever—and hokey TV commercials make you cry, it may be time to think about seeking some sort of help. If retail therapy and schlocky movie therapy don't do the job, consider professional counseling, Prozac, St. John's wort, a good glass of wine (not Ripple), a consultation with a Himalayan guru, crystal therapy, aromatherapy, color therapy, or aura therapy.

SANITY SAVERS (Do's)

9. Do plan for the departure. Have something specific planned to do with an empathetic someone right after your child leaves. Make reservations for dinner at the new restaurant you've been wanting to try. (Or if your austerity budget is already activated, a potluck picnic in the park with friends is an acceptable alternative.) Take a long walk with a bipedal friend. (Your dog is invited, but you'll need somebody with pockets for Kleenex.) Schedule a marathon-length session in a sensory deprivation tank. (Tell them to wake you in about six months.)

10. Do exercise regularly. Mind and body are connected. Find a way to keep this commitment. Get a workout buddy, or pay money to join a gym.

11. Do get a puppy now if you have a geriatric dog.

12. Do buy yourself fresh flowers once a week. (This is *not* just a girl thing.)

13. Do eat out more often. Justify this by thinking about the money you are saving on groceries. (Conveniently forget about that pesky tuition and room and board you're shelling out.) If your child is a boy, the difference might be substantial enough to allow you to dine at a four-star restaurant in Paris.

14. Do commit to attending a film festival or concert series, or buy season tickets to the theater or for athletic events. You now have the freedom to do so.

15. Do form a support group. Get together with other empty nesters; misery loves company. Talk, chat, yak, gab, schmooze, locute, communicate, discuss, discourse, prattle, confer, converse, rap, or, in New Age speak, engage, share, dialogue, process, do lunch.

16.

Do make a customized happy-music tape for when you feel a sadness attack coming on. Pick a theme song, and belt it out in your car or in the shower. You *will* feel better. Here are some upbeat ENS favorites that made their way onto our tape:

"Don't Worry, Be Happy" (Bobby McFerrin)
"Happy Talk" *(South Pacific)*
"I'm Free" (Rolling Stones)
"I'm Still Standing" (Elton John)
"It's My Turn" (Diana Ross)
"Oh, What a Beautiful Morning" *(Oklahoma!)*
"Peaceful Easy Feeling" (The Eagles)
"Respect" (Aretha Franklin)
"What a Day for a Daydream" (The Lovin' Spoonful)
"Whistle a Happy Tune" *(The King and I)*
"Zippity Doo Dah" *(Song of the South)*

17.

Do forge new, low-maintenance relationships with household appurtenances that can be left with a house sitter with a minimum of separation anxiety on your part. Silk houseplants and pet rocks are reasonable considerations.

Beware of goldfish, bonsai, and outdoor bird feeders. They are deceptively demanding.

18.

Do rent upbeat videos routinely. We guarantee you'll find something to cheer you up on our categorized list:

CLASSIC FUNNY
Duck Soup
The Graduate
His Girl Friday
The Odd Couple
The Pink Panther
A Shot in the Dark
When Harry Met Sally . . .
You Can't Take It with You

FOREIGN FUNNY
The Full Monty
La Cage aux Folles
Mama, There's a Man in Your Bed
My New Partner
Noises Off
The Visitors (2000)
any Monty Python film

FUNNY-FUNNY

All of Me (1984)
Bulworth
Dave
Dick
In and Out (1997)
Midnight Run
My Cousin Vinny
Outrageous Fortune
Ruthless People
Three Men and a Baby
What About Bob?

QUIRKY FUNNY

Beetlejuice
The Big Lebowski
Down and Out in Beverly Hills
Flirting with Disaster
I Love You to Death
The Muse
There's Something About Mary
any Woody Allen comedy

STUPID FUNNY

Ace Ventura: Pet Detective
Airplane
Animal House
Austin Powers: International Man of Mystery

Bill and Ted's Excellent Adventure
Billy Madison
Bowfinger
Caddyshack
Dumb and Dumber
A Fish Called Wanda
George of the Jungle
The Jerk
Pure Luck
Romancing the Stone
See No Evil, Hear No Evil
Stripes
The Three Amigos
Wayne's World
any Mel Brooks film

SWEET FUNNY
Bye Bye, Love
Crossing Delancey
Melvin and Howard
A New Leaf
Shakespeare in Love
Sixteen Candles
Tootsie
The Wedding

19.

Do talk to your own parents about how they coped with your departure.

 Don't get offended if they tell you that they popped a bottle of champagne and danced a jig when you walked out the door.

LET THE BAD TIMES ROLL (Was It Really All That Great?)

Reality checks are really important. In case your memory of the bad times fades, here are some useful blasts from the past that just might cheer you up:

20. Go to Toys "R" Us between Thanksgiving and Christmas. Spend at least thirty minutes fighting your way through the aisles and be sure to eavesdrop on a minimum of two parent-child interactions.

21. Offer to baby-sit the two-year-old from hell. Baby-sit the two-year-old from hell.

22. Borrow a really obnoxious, obscenity-ridden rap CD from one of your friends' kids. Crank up the volume.

23. Visit someone nine months pregnant during an August heat wave.

24. Build a pyramid of wet towels on the bathroom floor. Wait for the Mold Fairy to arrive.

25. Put childproof catches on the cabinets you use most frequently. (Leave them on a minimum of one week.)

26. Be diligent about appreciating not having to suffer through The Saturday Game. In the fall, wait for the most brutally inclement day, and go to a high-school soccer match. Take mental note of the hypothermic parent spectators just before leaving for the steamy warmth of the nearest Starbucks. Refresh your memory of how much you don't miss these activities in the spring. During a record-breaking heat wave, go to a Little League baseball game. Waltz through the bleachers, staying just long enough to relish the pervasive smell of sweat, the flushes of sunstroke, the tear- and dust-streaked players, and the escalating cacophony of parental belligerence. Leave for the lake.

27. Crawl out of bed at an uncivilized predawn hour and pretend you have to drive early-morning carpool. Dive back into bed and go to sleep again.

28. Set your alarm for 3:00 A.M. Establish the mood: She's an hour late, she hasn't called, and you don't know where she is. Now visualize: frantic pacing, listening for the car engine or the wail of the ambulance siren, the sneaky creaking of the bedroom window, your urge to call the emergency rooms of every hospital in the vicinity. We don't miss waiting up for her; neither will you.

29. Seize the opportunity, when at friends' houses, to indulge in vicarious nagging. Smugly sit back as you observe the parents standing with arms akimbo as they admonish their still-in-the-nest offspring to do their homework, clean their bedroom, get off the phone, or (God forbid) take out the trash.

EMOTIONAL PURGE (Let It All Hang Out)

Sometimes you just can't fight the sadness, so go with the flow. Indulge yourself in a good emotional purge. Unplug the phone and don't answer the door. There's nothing worse than reveling in a good depression, only to have it interrupted by a well-meaning, cheery friend. Include a time limit for each of these activities. This is a cathartic exercise, not a suicide mission.

30.

Darken the room, light a candle, get out the baby book, and put on one of the following appropriately sad songs:

"Already Gone" (The Eagles)
"The Circle Game" (Joni Mitchell)
"Cry on My Shoulder" (Bonnie Raitt)
"I'm So Lonesome I Could Cry" (Hank Williams)
"Just Call Out My Name" (Carole King)
"She's Leaving Home" (The Beatles)
"Sunrise, Sunset" (*Fiddler on the Roof*)
"Teen Angel" (Mark Dinning)
"Yesterday" (The Beatles)
any country-western song

31.

Buy enough Oreos for a satisfying binge (Godiva or Häagen-Dazs for the gourmet, carob chips for the health-conscious).

 Do not examine yourself naked in a full-length mirror afterward.

32.

Buy a large box of extra-soft Kleenex, and rent a truly sentimental movie. Any of the following would reduce even Rambo to tears:

Bambi
Beaches
E.T.—The Extra-Terrestrial
Ghost
The Ghost and Mrs. Muir
Heidi
The Lion King
Lorenzo's Oil
Love Story
Not Without My Daughter
Old Yeller
The Ryan White Story

CHAPTER 2

A Fresh Start *OR* It's Never Too Late

S ome of us are left-brained and some of us are right-brained. We all have a brain-side dominance that influences our choices of life activities, occupations, and leisure endeavors. Those who are left-brained tend to be more verbal and think in words, process information linearly, respond to logic, recall people's names, and apply the Pythagorean theorem to all aspects of daily life. Right-brainers tend to be more visual and think in images, process information in chunks, respond to emotion and intuition, recall people's faces, and think that the Pythagorean theorem is a Greek conspiracy to discredit aura reading.

There is convincing evidence that developing the untapped potential of the nondominant side of our brains has far-reaching benefits. Which brings us to the Nun Study, a study of 678 School Sisters of Notre Dame Congregation, a group of women known for their longevity, phenomenal mental and physical well-being, and statistically low incidence of Alzheimer's disease. These nuns kindly agreed to donate their brains to medical research upon their deaths. Laboratory analysis indicated that they had unusually minimal brain tissue deterioration for adults of their ages, which ranged from 75 to 103 years. An investigation into the sisters' activities revealed that they were constantly engaging in new tasks. To remind the nuns of the virtues of humility, their order advocated that they frequently be given jobs for which they had no skill. A culinary whiz might be assigned to a history-teaching detail. Scribes did a stint in the garden. The nuns' new activities stimulated the less-used, nondominant hemisphere of their brains. Instead of driving back and forth down the same experiential highway, they were building new roads, or neural pathways, in their brains.

So our point is, you can get through ENS and probably

deter brain sludge while you're at it if you put some well-thought-out energy into your Fresh Start. Many of us stay mentally and physically active, and that's important, but the key is to do more than just what you're good at or used to doing. Enjoy and broaden your current interests. Explore what you always wanted to do, and try something you never imagined yourself doing. Challenge yourself to step out of your physical, mental, and social comfort zones. Rather than doing this by having a torrid, adulterous affair, use our ensuing suggestions to do something constructive. Don't be intimidated because you think you'll be a total klutz when you make your debut on the tennis court, or that your first quiche will look like the effort of an unsupervised three-year-old. Instead, grin knowingly and think about the nuns and all the wonderful little neurons you're stimulating in your brain.

Unless you truly believe in reincarnation, the time for action is now. Don't procrastinate. Start by taking our 30-Second Left/Right Brain Survey, and use the results to pick activities glaringly outside of your comfort zone.

SCHAFFER AND WASSERMAN'S 30-SECOND LEFT/RIGHT BRAIN SURVEY

If, while looking at a pointillist painting by Georges Seurat, you start counting the dots, analyzing theories of color, and linking the relationship between the position of the dots and the automatic response of the optic nerve, you are definitely left-brained. Challenge yourself with creative writing, jazz drumming, or primal scream therapy.

If, upon opening a box of tools, you start waxing eloquently about the glint of sun on the patina of the surface of a wrench and its sensuous metallic curvature, you are incontrovertibly right-brained. Try repairing a watch, balancing your checkbook, or alphabetizing your books, CDs, cleaning products, snack foods, spices, videos, or vitamins.

MENTAL MASSAGE (Get Thinking)

33. Say to yourself, or better yet out loud, "I do not feel guilty for taking time for myself."

34. Treat yourself to a new magazine subscription—any mail is better than no mail. You won't believe what's out there:

American Cowboy
Bowling Digest
Car Stereo Review
Fast Company
Flex
Fur, Fish, and Game
Hockey Digest
Kiplinger's Retirement Report
Knitting Digest
New Jersey Monthly
Soap Opera Digest

35. Start playing the musical instrument you put away when the kids were born. Or pick up one you've always wanted to try. Who cares if you're not God's gift to Carnegie Hall or the Roxy?

36. Develop a talent you always envied, and sign up for lessons even if it's scary: singing, chain-saw sculpture, mandolin, woodworking, yodeling, beading, cake decorating.

37. Engage in activities that demand mental focus such as crossword puzzles, Boggle, Scrabble, chess, bridge, jacks.

38. Take a course in auto mechanics, sign language, creative writing, kite making, reflexology, calligraphy, welding, fencing, basic computer skills, or . . .

39. Learn a language in preparation for your dream vacation. Use cassettes if you're a commuter, or a CD-ROM if you're a computer nerd, or enroll in a class at your nearest adult education center—or even online.

40. Start catching up on your reading, but choose your books with care. Don't read anything too sad during the early clinical phases of ENS. Immerse yourself in one of these gems:

> *Angle of Repose* by Wallace Stegner (fiction)
> *Animal Dreams* by Barbara Kingsolver (fiction)
> *The Eight* by Katherine Neville (fiction)
> *The Endurance* by Caroline Alexander (nonfiction)
> *The House of the Spirits* by Isabel Allende
> (fiction)
> *Into Thin Air* by John Krakauer (nonfiction)
> *No Ordinary Time* by Doris Kearns Goodwin
> (nonfiction)
> *Rain of Gold* by Victor Villaseñor (nonfiction)
> *A Walk in the Woods* by Bill Bryson (nonfiction)
> *A Year in Provence* by Peter Mayle (nonfiction)

PHYSICAL FORAYS (Get Moving)

41. Do something involving equipment, such as kayaking, weight lifting, skiing, snowboarding, hang gliding, bicycling, rock climbing, surfing, windsurfing, tennis, golf, Ping-Pong, fishing, hunting, baseball, basketball, football, soccer, hockey, auto racing, polo, ice skating, in-line skating, roller-skating, cricket, skateboarding, Frisbee, rafting, scuba diving, canoeing, sailing, jump roping. Rent before you buy, or join a gym or club to test the waters. For pricey equipment, check out the classifieds, eBay, or other venues to scoop up slightly used stuff.

42. Do something that doesn't involve equipment: jogging, swimming, yoga, walking, karate, judo, tae kwan do, tai chi, wrestling, bird-watching, hiking, gardening, or any kind of dancing from African to zydeco.

SOCIAL STRIDES (Get Gregarious)

43. Start a book club. (This is *not* just a girl thing.) Call a diverse group of eight to twelve interesting, thoughtful people. Pick books by consensus, and then schedule monthly meetings to discuss each title. Here are some starter books guaranteed to keep the discussion lively:

Angela's Ashes by Frank McCourt (nonfiction)

For the Relief of Unbearable Urges by Nathan Englander (fiction)

Mama Day by Gloria Naylor (fiction)

Operating Instructions by Anne Lamott (nonfiction)

The Poisonwood Bible by Barbara Kingsolver (fiction)

Savages by Joe Kane (nonfiction)

The Spirit Catches You and You Fall Down by Anne Fadiman (nonfiction)

Their Eyes Were Watching God by Zora Neale Hurston (fiction)

Wild Swans by Jung Chang (nonfiction)

A Yellow Raft in Blue Water by Michael Dorris (fiction)

44. Join or start a gourmet group. For recipe ideas, go to the library, browse a bookstore, or visit the hundreds of foodie Web sites, such as *www.williamssonoma.com, www.epicurious.com*, or *www.splendidtable.com*.

45. Sign up for non-kid-oriented volunteer work, preferably something that doesn't require that you wear an unflattering smock. Options might include swinging a hammer for Habitat for Humanity, sharing your business expertise with fledgling entrepreneurs, working in local theaters or museums, teaching what you're good at, driving meals to shut-ins, doing hospital work (smock alert!), or for the adventurous who want to combine travel and volunteering, check out the Web site *www.globalvolunteers.org*.

46. Get a hobby that will put a new road map in your brain. Don't be afraid to go way out—check out handwriting analysis (be sure to read *Handwriting Analysis: Putting It To Work for You* by Andrea McNichol), investing in stocks and bonds, fire walking (this is more likely to put a new road map on the soles of your feet), photography, juggling, ham radios, Dumpster diving (there's actually a

Web site for this), quilting (it's never too early to subtly start applying pressure for grandchildren), soap making, rubber stamping, pottery, home brewing.

BEWARE THE WORK TRAP

Coffee overachievers that we baby boomers are, it's become quite the rage to take all that time freed up from carpooling, errand running, and nagging and transfer it neatly to the office. We've heard numerous tales of fellow empty nesters logging in the extra hours at work with the zeal of first-year medical residents—and we confess to some workaholic tendencies ourselves. Of course, if you tell us there's nothing that compares with the joys of plumbing the depths of your "in box," then by all means slog away. But is becoming a highly decorated workplace warrior what you really want? Why not validate your right to enjoy your newfound freedom? We strongly recommend that you give yourself a nudge and dare to delve into new territory.

NEW TRADITIONS (Get Adventurous)

47. Beware of kidless holidays. If you've always skied with your children on Thanksgiving, do something entirely different: Join your friends at the beach instead.

48. Put this book down right now, and go get a piece of paper and a pen. (See how easily we can get back in touch with our parent side?) Make a list of at least five things you absolutely want to do before you die. This is important goal setting.

49. Schedule a monthly massage (weekly if you can afford it).

50. Ask your friends about their favorite getaway spots. Go there.

51. Lighten up. Start swearing if you've always been a prim and proper language model, really *do* stop worrying, or pierce a hidden body part.

CHAPTER 3

You're Still a Parent OR It Ain't Over Yet

Get ready to parent in new and different ways. You are not exiting the parent role, you're just doing it differently. There are myriad ways to stay connected to your kids. They miss you too and will welcome your continued involvement, albeit on new terms. By which we mean, no stalking, spying, or other excessively clingy behavior.

LONG-DISTANCE PARENTING (Staying Connected)

52. Keep your finger on the pulse by being a great informer. (It's always okay to spy on other parents' kids.) Before your child leaves, be sure to get the phone numbers of his friends' parents. Call for updates about their kid and pass this info along to your child.

☞ Be sure to include news of surprise pregnancies, arrests, and enviable displays of child-to-parent devotion.

53. If your child is far way, reserve airline tickets as far ahead as possible. Some airlines allow you to book up to eleven months in advance. The Chanukah/Christmas season is the craziest, and there are limited seats. Don't put this one off.

 This is particularly essential if you are using frequent flyer miles.

54. The odds are, if she has wheels, she'll be driving a car that's in contention for the Most Miles and Duct Tape on a Still-Moving Vehicle award. Buy a little peace of mind and get AAA or other special insurance for road trips or the long drive home.

55. Plan on either attending the parent weekend or sending a surrogate. If finances or distance makes this prohibitive, be sure to send a package of homemade goodies and place a well-timed phone call.

56. Subscribe to any mailing list, newsletter, or newspaper from your child's college, service branch, or new locale.

57. E-mail is for everyone. Don't be intimidated if you're not technologically savvy. Ask for help. If you don't want to get a home account (hey, it's easy to do), use a friend's computer, the public library, or an Internet café, anywhere convenient and close by, to set up your free Hotmail (a type of e-mail) address. If your child is computerless, tell her to do the same.

58. Snail mail is not obsolete. There's something wonderful about finding a letter from home waiting in the mailbox.

59. Ensure your child's summer return by lining up a job possibility for her by April.

☞ If you want to discourage long summer stays, throw away the help-wanted ads.

60. Create opportunities to talk about your child; put a current picture on the fridge or a decal on your vehicle.

61. Buy T-shirts, key chains, coffee mugs, sweatshirts, anything naming your kid's new town or affiliation. It might be your most expensive purchase ever. ($20,000 a year tuition, and all you got was a lousy key chain?)

62. Start an emergency fund for a train or airline ticket to get to him as quickly as possible should the need arise. Think of this as an insurance policy you'll probably never need but wouldn't want to be without.

THE PHONE IS YOUR FRIEND
(Bankrolling an Industry)

Thank you, Alexander Graham Bell. Because of you, we have at our fingertips Touch-Tone phones, cordless phones, cell phones, pay phones, even dinosaur rotary phones, to keep the lines of communication open. It's a relatively cheap and effective tool to shorten the distance between you and your child.

63.
Establish a set time and day for regular phone calls. Be sure you and your child both feel comfortable with the frequency of the calls—not so often that the phone is a fiber-optic ball and chain, not so seldom that an unfamiliar voice says, "He moved three months ago."

64.
Send your child a phone card so that she can easily keep in touch with the important people in her life. It will be money well spent. You can purchase these cards at post offices, drugstores, or supermarkets.

65. Get an 800 number at home. Anyone can do this; just call 1-888-893-5094 for information.

66. For spontaneous quality calls, you may want to wait for him to call you. He's busy with his new life and will be more eager to talk if you don't interrupt a wild party or a "study date" in his room.

67. Use the phone to help celebrate her birthday long-distance style if you can't be there in person. Arrange a conference call with family members. (Dial 0 and ask the operator for help.) She could even open her presents while you're on the phone together. It's the next best thing to being in the same room.

68. Get a few phone numbers of your child's new acquaintances so that you have some contacts in case of an emergency. For example, if your child is sleeping off her first close encounter with a bottle of tequila, you will be able to alert her, via a friend, that Grandmother will be arriving in an hour for a surprise visit.

69.

Minimize your worries about your child's being stranded somewhere by buying him a for-emergency-only cell phone (and make him agree to pay anything over the basic monthly charges). You will have peace of mind knowing he has a safety net while walking home late at night or when dealing with a vehicular breakdown.

 Clearly explain that you do not consider ordering a pizza an emergency.

70.

Be a phone medic. When she calls home with the flu, tell her to grab her Get Well Kit (see number 90), recommend which items to use, and verbally tuck her into bed.

71.

Do not hesitate to use good old-fashioned guilt to keep the phone calls coming. On the answering machine that *you* bought her, leave a subtle message such as, "I haven't heard from you in over a week. For all I know you're lying dead in the horrible greenery outside your barracks. Call if this isn't true." Or, "Not that you care, but your father's having heart palpitations, I'm having debilitating migraines, and the cat is clinically depressed because you haven't bothered to call." What child wouldn't appreciate such thoughtfulness?

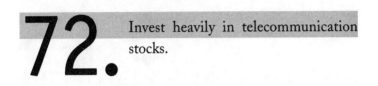

72. Invest heavily in telecommunication stocks.

CARE PACKAGES (Bubble Wrap Rocks)

Receiving a care package is guaranteed to make your kid's day. Package contents don't have to be dazzling, and a homemade one trumps the lame-o ones campus services provide. For ten dollars or less, you can put together a fun, creative, and practical surprise. Those everyday things (safety pins, dental floss, Chapstick) are always welcome. Constantly be on the lookout when shopping at markets or discount stores.

Use balance and variety when assembling your care package. Parents love to send pencils and Band-Aids; kids love to receive food and fun stuff. Remember the scene in the film *Dead Poets Society* when the kid used the contents of his care package—a disappointing desk set—as a Frisbee? Multiple sources report this is for real. Opening a package to find another box of stationery does not a happy kid make.

73.
It really helps to have a mental picture of his new living quarters. Immediately upon the departure of your baby, mail him a package containing a disposable camera, a prepaid return mailer, and his favorite cookies. Request he take pictures of his roommate(s), cafeteria or eating haunt, bedroom, and bathroom, to allow you to visualize his new surroundings.

Include a dire warning that no more cookies will be forthcoming until this assignment has been completed.

74.

When you send her birthday care package, include a cake that can survive the mail. If you're not Julia Child or Jacques Pepin, give yourself permission to order a Chocolate Decadence Cake from Harry and David's mail order catalog (call 1-800-547-3033). Don't forget the candles and a few balloons.

75.

Ensure that *you* get snail mail too. In each care package, include a self-addressed, stamped postcard to be mailed to you by your child.

76.

To attain superparent status, include a little something extra for the roommate(s) in the package, such as an extra Pez dispenser, a second container of spray string, or an additional Halloween decoration.

77. Start using Priority Mail mailers from the U.S. Post Office. They are free (except for the postage, of course) and easy to use and come in a variety of sizes.

78. You don't have to put your care package together all at once. Have an empty Priority Mailer on your desk, and keep adding to it.

79. Shop the day after a major holiday for random fun bargains. Pick up the ubiquitous Valentine conversation heart candy, tin bunny containers, Dracula candles, twinkly holiday lights, and paper turkey tablecloths.

80. Be a prepared care package parent. At all times have on hand the following materials: two-inch-wide clear packaging tape, permanent black markers, bubble wrap, and an assortment of those Priority Mailers.

81. Organize a care package party by getting together with seven other ENS parents. Each parent brings eight of the same item and a packing box. Have packaging materials on hand. For an extra treat, have the parents write to one another's children. Include the letters.

82. And then there's the "after the visit home" phone call she makes within moments of returning to her "other" home. Expect to hear fifteen seconds of "I love you, you're wonderful, I miss you already," followed by heart-wrenching pleas to send such indispensable forgotten items as (a) her roommate's borrowed designer jacket that's under her bed; (b) the hair-streaking kit that he didn't get around to buying during his two months home; (c) the scrubby thing in the shower (no doubt now mildewed); (d) the four favorite CDs he left at his girlfriend's house (the one who lives way out in the country).

 Don't be caught unprepared for this predictable call. Be sure to have a large Priority Mailer addressed and ready to pack.

83. Crumbs are crummy to receive. Put goodies in hard plastic containers padded with generous amounts of bubble wrap, and send baked treats that will survive the journey and arrive intact. We gastronomically recommend Judith's Snappy Gingersnaps, Lauren's Chocolate Swirl Brownies, and Glory's Glorious Lemon Bars.

 Make extra so that some actually make it into the care package.

Judith's Snappy Gingersnaps

¾ cup butter
1 cup white sugar
1 egg
¼ cup molasses
2 cups flour
2 teaspoons baking soda
½ teaspoon salt
2 tablespoons powdered ginger
2 teaspoons cinnamon
extra sugar for rolling

1. Preheat oven to 350° F.
2. Mix all of the ingredients together.
3. Roll into 1-inch balls; roll the balls in the sugar.
4. Place the balls on a greased pan, two inches apart.
5. Bake for 10 to 12 minutes, until the tops crack.
6. Let cool.

Makes 4 dozen 2-inch cookies

(Optional: a pinch of cayenne, or a teaspoon of cut-up crystallized ginger)

Lauren's Luscious Chocolate Swirl Brownies

1 cup butter

1½ cups brown sugar

2 eggs

1 teaspoon baking soda

1 teaspoon vanilla extract

½ teaspoon salt

2¼ cup white sifted flour

12-oz package semisweet chocolate chips

1. Preheat oven to 350° F.
2. Cream the butter and brown sugar together with a wooden spoon.
3. Add the eggs, baking soda, vanilla, and salt. Mix well.
4. Add the flour. Mix well.
5. Put the mixture in a greased 9×13-inch baking pan, and spread evenly. Pour the chocolate chips evenly over the top. Bake for 4 minutes. Then take a knife and swirl the melted chips through the brownies. Bake for an additional 12 to 14 minutes. Let cool before cutting.

Makes approximately 20 brownies

Glory's Glorious Lemon Bars

$\frac{1}{2}$ cup butter
$\frac{1}{4}$ cup powdered sugar
1 cup plus 2 tablespoons flour
pinch salt
2 eggs, beaten
2 tablespoons lemon juice
1 cup sugar
zest from $\frac{1}{2}$ lemon

1. Preheat oven to 350°F.
2. Combine the butter, powdered sugar, 1 cup flour, and salt with your hands, or cut together using two knives. Line the bottom and sides of an 8×8-inch pan with a thin layer of mixture.
3. Bake this shell for 15 to 20 minutes.
4. Mix the eggs, lemon juice, sugar, 2 tablespoons flour, and lemon zest. Pour the mixture into the baked shell.
5. Return to the oven for 20 to 25 minutes.
6. When cool, sprinkle with additional powdered sugar.

Makes 16 bars

HOW TO STUFF A WILD CARE PACKAGE

Below is a two-pronged approach to the fine art of select-
ing care package items. We have included general lists by
category, as well as theme package ideas.

GENERAL ITEMS

84. **Stock up on these practical items:**
pens; pencils; Post-its (designer and
multicolored are winners); liquid paper
correction pen; Wite-Out; envelopes; self-addressed,
stamped envelopes (for the more hopeful); self-addressed,
stamped postcards (for the less wordy); stamps; film;
Scotch tape; batteries; glue sticks; paper clips; extension
cords; small stapler and staples; and thumbtacks. (Don't
bother sending hangers—your kid can buy ten for a dollar at any discount store.)

85. **Keep your child looking spiffy and
smelling good:** soap, lotions (hand,
face, body, feet), Q-tips, shampoo and
conditioner, dental floss, disposable razors or blades,
toothpaste and toothbrush, deodorant, concentrated
breath freshener, sunscreen, back scrubber, nylon body

scrubber, clean-pore strips, nail file, nail clippers, after-shave (for guys), nail polish and hair clips and ties (for girls).

86. **Here's a good start for first-aid needs:** cough drops; small packets of Kleenex (better than dorm toilet paper for a cold); aspirin; ibuprofen or Tylenol; antibiotic ointment; Chapstick; Band-Aids; and an Ace bandage. For extra credit, toss in an antihistamine (get the no-drowsy formula) and some kind of stomach soother (for those 3:00 A.M. pizza binges).

87. **Food is always welcome:** tea bags; snack crackers; instant cold drink powders and a Rubbermaid container; Nutri-Grain bars; PowerBars; granola bars; soup-in-a-cup; miso soup packets; tuna kits; microwave popcorn; Payday bars (peanuts provide cleverly disguised protein); beef/turkey jerky; fruit roll-ups; hot chocolate packets; cans of instant flavored coffees; sucky-chewy stuff like gum, Life Savers, hard candy, or Tic-Tacs; peanut brittle; dried apricots; and homemade baked goods (pumpkin bread and banana bread ship well).

88.

Even big kids need to play. These items have been dorm-tested: fake tattoos, bubble gum, Mad-Libs, blank cassettes, mini Nerf footballs, Frisbees, decks of cards, Superballs, Pez and dispenser, bubbles, Slinky, paddle-balls, jacks, junky magazines, novelty stationery, stickers (you're never too old), poker chips, Koosh balls, Hacky Sacks, action figures (or other stupid stuff), Silly Putty, water pistols (brightly colored, at least two), origami paper, and back-scratchers.

89.

Every once in a while, succumb to your urge to splurge: something silk (we enthusiastically recommend boxers, pillowcases, and sleeping bags from Dreamsack; contact them at 1-800-670-7661 or on their Web site at *www.dreamsack.com*), new CDs, Itty Bitty book lights (to keep peace among roommates), phone cards, pizza money, a new clothing surprise, a new or favorite videotape, or a twenty-dollar bill (always welcome).

IDEAS FOR THEME PACKAGES

90. **The Get Well Kit:** cough drops, lotion-permeated Kleenex, vitamin C, Mama Bear's Cold Care tea (Celestial Seasonings), package of dried chicken soup, commercial cold medication, Chap Stick, and a small teddy bear.

91. **The Room Decor Inspiration:** wind chimes, framed family picture, stick-mount hooks, towel hooks, over-the-door hooks (to increase clothes-hanging potential), poster putty, small dry-erase message board and pen, glow-in-the-dark stars, small white Christmas lights, small candles (where permitted), Indian bedspreads or sarongs (multipurpose), prism for window, seasonal holiday decorations, and potpourri or other good-smelling stuff to override the scent of ripening workout clothes.

92. **The Clothing Rescue:** lint roller, stain-remover stick, quarters for laundry (heavy but fun), safety pins, small sewing kit, new socks, dryer softener sheets, and travel packets of laundry detergent.

93. **The Friend or Roomie Birthday Box:** Nerf ball, wrapping paper, Scotch tape, ribbon, and generic birthday card.

94. **The Road Trip Express:** travel-sized packages of deodorant, shampoo, and conditioner; aspirin; disposable razor;

toothbrush and toothpaste; gas money or gas card; disposable camera; map of the entire United States; custom cassette tape of favorite music from a local radio station or the family collection; chocolate-covered espresso beans; and Visine.

95.

The Stress Survival Special: Tums, medicated acne cream, canker sore gel, Tension Tamer tea (Celestial Seasonings), Instant Meal bar, mini Nerf ball, deck of cards, chocolate-covered espresso beans, aromatherapy candles, meditation tape, CD of soothing music, crayons and coloring books, and condoms (you're not as liberal as you thought you were, are you?).

MONEY (As If You Had Any Left)

The good news is, you're still a parent. The bad news is, it's still expensive. According to statistics, it costs approximately $200,000 to raise your child from birth to age eighteen. Don't start counting spare cash now that they're gone. If your kids are in college or moving into their first home, you're probably teetering on the brink of bankruptcy. Keep your sense of humor and take fiscal action.

96. Apply for an airline mileage credit card. Each dollar spent equals one mile. These cards are available through airlines, credit card companies, banks, and professional organizations. Put everything you can on this credit card, and use these valuable miles to bring your kids home or to visit them.

97. Make sure to avoid outlandish credit card payments when accruing your miles. Here is a tried-and-true technique to avoid cardiac arrest when opening your bill: Keep all credit card receipts for the billing period in an envelope. Every Sunday, total the amount for the week, write a check to the credit company for your week's expenditures, put the check and receipts back in the envelope. When your bill comes at the end of the month, mail the four checks.

98. For those of you who own a house with equity, take out a low-interest loan to pay off your credit card debt or to help pay for your child's expenses.

99. Maximize mileage opportunities. Let friends and coworkers (not ones in competition for miles) know you would love to put their big-ticket purchases on your card and have them pay the cash to you.

100. Pay college tuition with your mileage credit card.

101. Join an investment club, or go to *www.better-investing.org,* the Web site for the National Association of Investors Corporation. Its goal is to help people learn to invest in the stock market. It's never too late to get smart about your money.

102. Have a five-year travel plan. Start a fund for a dream trip. Enlist a travel partner now.

KEEPING KIDS IN YOUR LIFE (Don't Go Overboard!)

Stay involved with other people's kids. The beauty of surrogate parenting is that you get to pick and choose your level of commitment. Politely decline to take the hormone-riddled fifteen-year-old to her appointment with her probation officer. Enthusiastically volunteer to travel to Washington, D.C., with your best friend's son who has just won an all-expenses-paid trip for himself and a chaperone.

103. Be a prom mom or, like, a totally rad dad for a friend's or a relative's kid.

104. Adopt a kid for a weekend.

 Firmly establish departure time.

105.

Be a safe haven for your best friend's son who is driving her crazy. Let him know he's more than welcome for *one* meal, *one* shower, and *one* night.

 If said son appears with suitcase in hand, rescind offer immediately.

106.

Offer to take a friend's child out for a driving lesson.

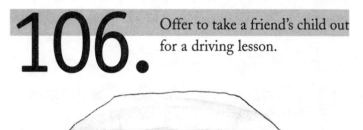

Be sure it's their car, not yours.

 Verify that your hospitalization insurance is current.

 Self-medicate before getting in the passenger seat (aka death seat).

 **107.** Invite a foreign exchange student for dinner or an interesting outing.

 Do *not* commit to having a foreign exchange student live with you immediately after your last child leaves home. Allow yourself time to get used to your empty nest.

108. Volunteer to help an elementary-school student who's struggling with math. You will garner high praise and heroic tutor status if you use the book *Number Jugglers* by Ruth Bell Alexander.

109.

Attend school plays, concerts, and sports activities with friends whose kids are still in high school.

 Refer to number 26, should conditions not be optimal.

CHAPTER 4

The Visitor Returns *OR* The Nest Is Full Again . . . Sort Of

The first visit home will begin a new chapter in your parent-child relationship. The anticipation and excitement of his return will be accompanied by new issues and expectations on both sides. This is a wonderful opportunity to begin to get to know your child as a young adult. You will always be his parent and he will always be your child, but the potential to relate to him as an adult can be exciting, scary, and mutually rewarding.

NEW ISSUES (Who, Me? Rules?)

110. Your child has been living without parental supervision. With that comes independence. Sit down and have a talk about your expectations and hers for the visit home. Find *your* comfort zone, not hers, but do so tactfully. You really *do* want her to come home. You really *don't* want her to bring her boyfriend home for the summer.

111. Set clear ground rules. Here are some issues you can anticipate:

Is there a curfew?

Will "significant others" be staying overnight, and if so, what will the sleeping arrangements be?

Are there certain household chores you expect him to do?

If she will be working, are there any financial expectations you have of her?

Do you expect him home for dinner?

Does she have unlimited access to the car, the
liquor cabinet, your closet, and your ATM
account?

Does he need to check in with you about coming
home at night, or let you know if he's sleeping elsewhere?

112.

If, for the first three days of his
visit, all you have seen of him
are his suitcases, which are still
in the middle of the living room, minus his dirty clothes,
which miraculously made it to the laundry room for your
personalized attention, it's time to call a pro. Your Jewish
friends are culturally programmed experts in the field of
guilt, with an endless source of prompts. Here's one for
the laundry problem:

> "So, don't worry, (*insert child's name here*), I'll do
> the washing while you're sleeping so the machine
> noise shouldn't annoy you (and so, God forbid, if
> you should get in an accident, you won't be wear-
> ing dirty underwear)."

Your Catholic comrades will be rich fonts of spiritual
advice. Ask them to help connect you to the right patron
saint—regardless of your religious persuasion. Saint
George protects against Herpes, Saint Angela of Foligno

(and seven others—it's a big job) patrols against Sexual
Temptation, and our personal favorite, Saint Mathilda,
provides the panacea for Disappointing Children.

LETTING GO (Hi, I'm Home, Love Ya, Gotta Go!)

113.

Accept the fact that it's never the same after he leaves. He returns as a visitor. He's different and so are you.

114.

Do not take personally her overwhelming desire to reconnect with friends instead of cozying up to you for a long pajama-clad chat. As if you really wanted to hear more about how, on a dare, she pulled the dorm fire alarm, causing ten thousand students to stand shivering on the quad at midnight. (Being privy to this knowledge would, of course, explain the impressive amount of "volunteer work" she's been doing.)

115.

In getting ready for his return, be sure that the pathway from the front door to the telephone is unencumbered so as to preempt the possibility of broken furniture or broken bones.

116. Avoid falling back into old nagging patterns. Express gratitude if you can see any bare or unoccupied area of her bedroom floor. Ignore your favorite coffee mug, now the breeding ground for an unidentifiable blue, noxious, scummy substance.

117. When asked, at 11:00 P.M. the night before his imminent departure, to wash his composting pile of laundry, assume a martyrlike attitude and agree. Go the extra mile, and iron everything. Then, as you lovingly hand-deliver the carefully folded clothes, ask yourself, *Will I really miss this?*

118. Be prepared for the sadness that will accompany her redeparture. This is the time to remind yourself that the glass is half full. (We give you permission to fill the wineglass all the way full.) Put your music back on the reclaimed stereo, call a friend on your liberated phone line, or just enjoy the quiet.

SEIZE THE MOMENT (Carpe Diem)

119. Be flexible and celebrate when you can. Have your family Thanksgiving meal in June, your Passover seder in July, or your Christmas dinner in August, when everyone is together.

120. Schedule specific times for family activities, and give your child advance warning that these are unbreakable commitments and cannot be superseded by last-minute invitations to a Dave Matthews concert. Don't be afraid to remind him that *you* paid for the ticket home.

121. Revamp old traditions. The weeklong family vacation may have to be shortened to two days due to kids' work schedules or other commitments.

122.

To ensure more time with your child, invite her friends along on outings, welcome them for holiday vacations, and keep a well-stocked pantry for her drop-in dinner guests.

123. A progressive dinner is an excellent way to see your child's friends as well as guarantee the presence of your own child the evening of the event. Each family prepares one course of the meal and the kids rotate from house to house. Keep the camera ready. The pictures will be a great addition to a postvisit care package.

CHAPTER 5

Senior Year Revisited *OR* Hindsight Is 20/20

Looking back, you may realize that the actual moment of the long-dreaded departure wasn't as devastating as anticipated. In reality, you had been in the throes of ENS for the whole year prior to her actual migration. If you had known then what you know now, you could have been more proactive about channeling those separation pangs into constructive activities. Here are some things we wished we had done for kid number one. Use your new wisdom to prepare for the departure of your next child, or pass on what you've learned to your friends with high-school seniors.

124. Keep a loaded camera or charged video camera on hand at all times (disregard the groans) to document the senior year. Not only will he love showing the pictures to his new friends, but he will be sure to occasionally remember his past life.

125. Volunteer at the high school for senior year activities. *Do* be selective. Offer to stuff envelopes for the tea honoring parents of valedictorians and salutatorians. *Don't* chaperone dances unless you're ready for your kid to petition for early emancipation. *Never* volunteer for any clean-up committee—it will leave you with little hope for the future of our planet.

126. Take Kleenex to even the most seemingly innocent senior year events. You never know what might trigger an ENS episode: the last football game, the last concert, the last parent-teacher conference, the last visit with the truancy officer. . . .

127.

If you can help it, don't get involved in obsessive projects like building or renovating a house, writing a book, researching a family genealogy, or running for public office during her last year at home.

128.

Put together a photo album, a videotape, or a slide show that is a documentary of your child's life. (It's easy to have prints made into slides.) Although

the creative process will be frequently interrupted by hysterical crying jags, this yearlong activity will help you accept the fact that she's leaving, while providing her with a treasured gift. If you have a scanner or digital camera, you can put photos online so she can visit them with the click of a mouse.

129. Make a quilt. If you are a stitch wizard, a compulsive pack rat, and an overachiever, you'll be able to piece together scraps of everything he's outgrown since the age of one. It's the perfect excuse to finally purge your linen closet of the Power Ranger pillowcase.

130. If you're no Martha Stewart, buy a plain quilt, take it to all social functions (again, ignore the groans), and have family members and friends embroider or fabric-pen their names and a special message on it. This quilt will add a touch of home to her new room.

131. Get your mileage credit card at the beginning of his senior year so that you'll have plenty of miles to fly him home for the first visit.

132.

Plan a last family fling. Depending upon your budget, it can be anything from camping to the Caribbean. This is a serious bonding opportunity. Resist all impulses to remind him to brush his teeth, quit picking his nose, stand up straight, or get the hair out of his eyes so you can see his gorgeous face. Call us wusses, but bring lots of gin and tonic—you'll need it.

133.

Bolster your daily vitamin regimen with a *really strong* antidepressant if you can talk your doctor into it.

☞ WARNING—DANGER—CAVEAT—BEWARE

Some of us (definitely the less fortunate) who have been through an empty nest experience learned about the potential for Explosive Emotional Chemical Spills that may occur during the month/week/days before they leave.

As you are entertaining wishful thoughts of luring your departing six-footer over to his baby book for a sentimental farewell, he may be gearing up for his transition to uncharted independence by subconsciously sabotaging your tender predeparture scenarios. Inexplicable behaviors (nothing new, of course) might seem to increase exponentially as D-Day (Departure Day) approaches, the formula being: IA—Irrational Action—is inversely proportionate to DLN—Days Left in the Nest. Or the closer *it* gets, the worse *he* gets. This is because there is an obnoxious switch built into teenagers, timed to go off precisely when parents need help kicking them out of the nest.

You are entering a passive (or not so passive)-aggressive minefield, fueled by your child's simultaneous need for emancipation and fear of separation. Her love for you may be well camouflaged by particularly nasty behavior. Also, she will be warming up to her upcoming absentee status by increasing her time away from home. Consider yourself lucky if she even occasionally graces you with her presence at the dinner table. Better yet, purchase and install a convict-tracking device on her ankle so that you at least know where she is.

Expectations for a fond farewell scene should be kept to a minimum. Be prepared for furtive glances and eye-rolling when you meet the roommate(s). Your child is living in fear that you will say "cool" or "neat," unthinkingly hum Mr. Rogers's theme song, talk about cow tipping, start dancing the macarena, or worse yet, take off your oversize sunglasses to reveal your bloodshot, puffy, tear-filled eyes. Basically, think of the entire departure process as a "duck and cover" drill. Put your head down and protect what you can; hindsight assures us that this, too, shall pass.

CHAPTER 6

You're Getting Over ENS When . . .

Certain behaviors will herald your approach to the eighth and final phase of Empty Nest Syndrome: glee. Your shifting perspective from grief to relief, from tears to cheers may catch you off-guard, making it difficult to recognize this transition. Therefore we have provided sample indicators to help you recognize this momentous passage.

YOU'RE GETTING OVER ENS WHEN . . .

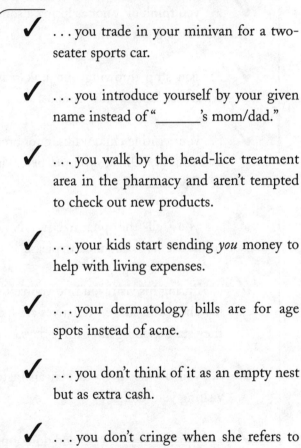

✔ . . . you trade in your minivan for a two-seater sports car.

✔ . . . you introduce yourself by your given name instead of "_____'s mom/dad."

✔ . . . you walk by the head-lice treatment area in the pharmacy and aren't tempted to check out new products.

✔ . . . your kids start sending *you* money to help with living expenses.

✔ . . . your dermatology bills are for age spots instead of acne.

✔ . . . you don't think of it as an empty nest but as extra cash.

✔ . . . you don't cringe when she refers to her new residence as "home."

✓ . . . you can drive by his elementary or high school and not need to listen to your "happy tape." (We'd rather forget the junior high years.)

✓ . . . you think of it not as losing a son but as gaining a guest room.

✓ . . . you stop throwing out junk mail that advertises "adults only" condos.

✓ . . . your visiting child walks in for breakfast, and you say, "Oh, are you *still* here?" instead of "Good morning."

✓ . . . you tell the pharmacist, "No more (expletive) childproof caps, please."

✓ . . . during his visit, you find yourself thinking about the adage, "Relatives are like fish; they start spoiling after three days."

✓ . . . you decide to go to Hawaii instead of visiting your child.

✓ . . . you screen your calls and do not pick up when you hear your kid's voice asking for money.

✓ . . . you hear the Beatles song "Yesterday," and the first thing you think of is that you forgot to pick up your jacket at the dry cleaners yesterday.

✓ . . . you look at your kid's kindergarten painting and think to yourself, "Why in the world have I kept this for thirteen years?" and into the trash it goes.

✓ . . . you stop drinking your wine out of his Tommy-Tippee cup.

✓ . . . you replace the college car decal with the bumper sticker "Eve Was Framed."

✓ . . . your second phone line is for the computer, not your teenager.

✓ . . . you're looking forward to getting mail from AARP instead of the PTA.

✓ . . . you tell her you'll call her back after *Ally McBeal* is over.

✓ . . . you hear a baby cry in a restaurant, and instead of saying, "Oh, the poor thing," you have surprisingly insensitive thoughts such

✓ as, "Why doesn't someone stuff a sock in that kid's mouth?"

✓ . . . instead of crying when he leaves after a prolonged visit, you present him with an itemized bill for rent, long-distance phone calls, laundry, food, professional fumigation of his bedroom, gas, wear-and-tear on your vehicle, and wear-and-tear on you.

✓ . . . you tell your kid to get her own damned car insurance.

✓ . . . you're looking forward to the extra hangers.

✓ . . . you reallocate your antidepressant budget for a house cleaner.

✓ . . . you mail him the things he forgot after a visit home via C.O.D. instead of FedEx.

✓ . . . you can confidently stand up and happily declare, "My name is _____ and I am a recovering empty nester."

✓ . . . you can write a book about Empty Nest Syndrome to give advice to others.

INDEX

ABOUT THE AUTHORS

LAUREN AND SANDY

- have been married (not to each other) for fifty-one years

- have four kids, two husbands, two indulged dogs, and four cats

- pledge allegiance to Bruce Springsteen, David Grisman, and Joni Mitchell

- will drive six hours for a concert

- believe chocolate is a food group and a meal without garlic is a meal without sunshine

- unplug the phone and hang out the Do Not Disturb sign during the World Series

- were friends for eighteen years before realizing they could write together

- would be perfectly proportioned if a foot taller

- plan on having great singing voices in their next lifetimes

- hate rodents and spiders

- have traveled with their kids to every continent except Antarctica and Australia

- can communicate in English, French, American Sign Language, Spanish, and a little Bahasan, and know the word for "pizza" in Italian

- have two B.A.'s, three M.A.'s, and enough postgrad credits for a Ph.D. in something

- hold real jobs

- have taught more than 8,003 students, both young and old

- are deserving of Olympic Gold for surviving over forty years of parenting

- have found the perfect balance in life—a small mountain town (Ashland, Oregon) as a home base and a passion for traveling to countries with great food (the British Isles are out) and world-class museums

- are surviving Empty Nest Syndrome and are shamelessly allocating increasingly larger proportions of their meager discretionary income to adult endeavors